Heinemann First ENCYCLOPEDIA

Volume 6
Ind-Lic

Heinemann Library
Chicago, Illinois

© 1999, 2006 Heinemann Library
a division of Reed Elsevier Inc.
Chicago, Illinois

Customer Service   888–454–2279

Visit our website at www.heinemannlibrary.com

Series Editors: Rebecca and Stephen Vickers, Gianna Williams
Author Team: Rob Alcraft, Catherine Chambers, Sabrina Crewe, Jim Drake, Fred Martin, Angela Royston, Jane Shuter, Roger Thomas, Rebecca Vickers, Stephen Vickers

This revised and expanded edition produced for Heinemann Library by Discovery Books.
Photo research by Katherine Smith and Rachel Tisdale
Designed by Keith Williams, Michelle Lisseter, and Gecko
Illustrations by Stefan Chabluk and Mark Bergin

Originated by Ambassador Litho Limited
Printed in China by WKT Company Limited

10 09 08 07 06
10 9 8 7 6 5 4 3 2

Library of Congress Cataloging-in-Publication Data

Heinemann first encyclopedia.
       p.   cm.
     Summary: A fourteen-volume encyclopedia covering animals, plants, countries, transportation, science, ancient civilizations, US states, US presidents, and world history
     ISBN 1-4034-7113-4 (v. 6 : lib. bdg.)
     1.   Children's encyclopedias and dictionaries.
   I. Heinemann Library (Firm)
   AG5.H45 2005
   031—dc22   2005006176

Acknowledgments
Cover: Cover photographs of a desert, an electric guitar, a speedboat, an iceberg, a man on a camel, cactus flowers, and the Colosseum at night reproduced with permission of Corbis. Cover photograph of the Taj Mahal reproduced with permission of Digital Stock. Cover photograph of an x-ray of a man, and the penguins reproduced with permission of Digital Vision. Cover photographs of a giraffe, the Leaning Tower of Pisa, the Statue of Liberty, a white owl, a cactus, a butterfly, a saxophone, an astronaut, cars at night, and a circuit board reproduced with permission of Getty Images/Photodisc. Cover photograph of Raglan Castle reproduced with permission of Peter Evans; J. Allan Cash Ltd, pp. 9, 10, 11, 13 top, 15, 18, 19, 23, 24 top, 30, 35, 37, 47; AFP/Getty Images, p. 31 bottom; Glen Allison/Stone, p. 29; Ancient Art and Architecture, p. 12; Bettman/Corbis, p. 21 bottom; Corbis, p. 43 bottom; C. Borland/PhotoLink, p. 46 bottom; Breslich and Foss, p. 33; Bridgeman Art Library, p. 42 bottom; BBC Natural History Unit/Brian Lightfoot p. 5 top; Bruce Coleman/Trevor Barrett, p. 40 top; Mary Kate Denny, p. 38; Hulton Deutsch, p. 4; T.E. Clarke, p. 16; Alfred Eisenstaedt/Time Life Pictures/Getty Images, p. 28 top; Getty Images, p. 25 top; Chris Johnson, p. 41; Hulton Archive/Getty Images, p. 45; Lisa Taylor, p. 24 bottom; Jazz Photo Library/Christian Him, p. 20 top; Peter Newark, p. 42 top; Oxford Scientific Films, pp. 5 bottom, 48 bottom; Alan and Sandy Carey, p. 17 bottom; Kenneth Day, p. 34 top; Douglas Faulkner, p. 14 top; MPL Fogden, p. 7; Frances Furlong, p. 44 top; Frank Huber, p. 14 bottom; Breck Kent, p. 22 top; Renee Lynn, p. 17 top; Tom McHugh, p. 32 top; Joyce Naltchayan/AFP/Getty Images, p. 25 bottom; Peter Parks, pp. 22 bottom, 48 bottom; Tui de Roy, p. 32 bottom; Kjell Sandved, p. 34 bottom; Paul Schutzer/Time Life Pictures/Getty Images, p. 28 bottom; Richard Shiell, p. 36 bottom; Lee Snider/Photo Images/Corbis, p. 46 top; Stock Montage/Getty Images, p. 21 top; Victoria Stone, p. 44 bottom; Redferns, p. 20 bottom; Scenics of America/PhotoLink, p. 8; Science Photo Library/NASA, p. 39 top; Stone, p. 27; Mike Theiler/Getty Images, p. 43 top; Philippe Plailly, p. 39 bottom; Trip, p. 13 bottom.

Welcome to
Heinemann First Encyclopedia

What is an encyclopedia?

An encyclopedia is an information book. It gives the most important facts about many different subjects. This encyclopedia has been written for children who are using an encyclopedia for the first time. It covers many of the subjects from school and others you may find interesting.

What is in this encyclopedia?

In this encyclopedia, each topic is called an *entry*. There is one page of information for every entry. The entries in this encyclopedia explain

- animals
- plants
- dinosaurs
- countries
- geography
- history
- world religions
- music
- art
- transportation
- science
- technology
- states
- famous Americans

How to use this encyclopedia

This encyclopedia has thirteen books called *volumes*. The first twelve volumes contain entries. The entries are all in alphabetical order. This means that Volume 1 starts with entries that begin with the letter A and Volume 12 ends with entries that begin with the letter Z. Volume 13 is the index volume. It also has other interesting information.

Here are two entries that show you what you can find on a page:

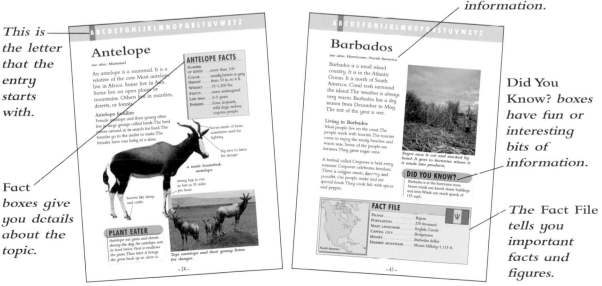

This is the letter that the entry starts with.

Fact boxes give you details about the topic.

The "see also" line tells you where to find other related information.

Did You Know? boxes have fun or interesting bits of information.

The Fact File tells you important facts and figures.

Industrial Revolution

see also: United Kingdom

An industrial revolution is when factory machines begin to make things quickly. Many people begin to work in factories. Before an industrial revolution, people made things by hand. Most of the people were farmers.

The first industrial revolution

The first industrial revolution began in Britain in about 1750. Machines were invented that could spin and weave cloth quickly. The first machines were powered by water or operated by people. Then machines were driven by steam power. Coal was burned to make the steam.

KEY DATES

Different countries had industrial revolutions at different times in their histories.

1750s	Britain becomes industrialized.
1850s	Belgium, France, Germany, and the U.S.A. become industrialized.
1880s	Sweden and Japan become industrialized.
1900s	Russia and China become industrialized.
1950s	Parts of South America, Asia, and Africa become industrialized.

The revolution spreads

Other countries found out how Britain made things with machines. They copied these machines. They made the machines better. They had their own industrial revolutions.

These machines were used to spin cotton during the industrial revolution in Britain.

Insect

see also: Animal, Invertebrate, Metamorphosis

An insect is a small invertebrate. It has six legs. It has a hard covering around its body. Insects are common everywhere. They are on land, in the air, and in water.

Insect families

Most insects hatch from eggs that are laid by an adult female. A young insect is called a larva. The larva can look very different from the adult. The larva becomes a pupa. The pupa changes into an adult insect. The body of an adult insect has three parts. The three parts are the head, thorax, and abdomen. Some insects live together in groups called communities. Other insects live alone.

PLANT AND INSECT EATER

Some insects feed on plants. Others eat other animals. An insect either chews or sucks its food.

INSECT FACTS

NUMBER OF	
KINDS	more than 10 million
COLOR	often black, brown, or green
LENGTH	up to 4 inches
LIFE SPAN	usually less than a year
ENEMIES	birds, spiders, snakes, other animals, people

The green tiger beetle looks just like a green leaf. This helps it hide.

hard skin gives the insect its shape

one or two pairs of wings

antennae to smell and feel

big eyes to see anything that moves

holes in the sides of the body for breathing

a desert locust

Internet

see also: Communication, Computer, Telephone

The Internet is a way of connecting computers together. Computers anywhere in the world can send and receive information using the Internet. The World Wide Web is part of the Internet.

How does the Internet work?

The Internet started with a few powerful computers. The computers were connected. They could pass information to each other very quickly.

Now, personal computers (PCs) can be connected to the Internet using a modem. The modem helps to send messages along telephone lines. The messages go to a service provider. The service provider has a powerful computer. This computer passes the messages along to other computers.

Companies, organizations, and individual people can put information on websites or home pages. The information can be about anything. Computers everywhere can get this information through the Internet.

DID YOU KNOW?

E-mail is the short name for electronic mail. E-mail can be used just like mailing a letter. E-mail on the Internet sends messages between computers.

The Kennedy Space Center website gives up-to-date information about the United States space program.

Invertebrate

see also: Crustacean, Insect, Mollusk, Vertebrate

An invertebrate is an animal that has no bones inside its body. Worms, jellyfish, snails, crabs, and insects are all invertebrates. Invertebrates are found everywhere in the world.

PLANT, INSECT, AND MEAT EATER

Different invertebrates eat different kinds of plants or animals. The shape of an invertebrate's mouth and body helps it to catch and eat the kind of food it likes.

Invertebrate families

Most invertebrates have several stages in their lives. A young invertebrate hatches out of an egg. It might not look like the adult. Most invertebrates are male or female. Some are both male and female at the same time.

This is a banana slug. This invertebrate has no shell or hard covering to protect its soft body.

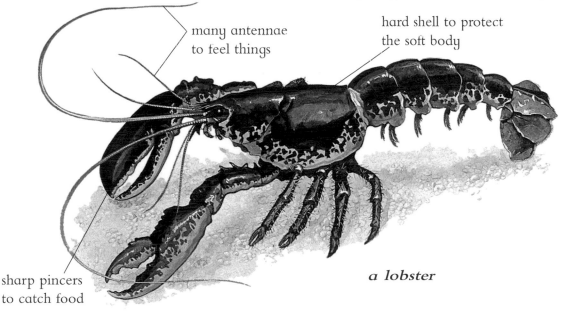

many antennae to feel things

hard shell to protect the soft body

sharp pincers to catch food

a lobster

Iowa

see also: United States of America

Iowa is a state in the central United States of America. Rivers border Iowa on both sides—the Missouri River on the west and the Mississippi River on the east. The soil in Iowa is rich. It makes the best farmland in the United States. Winters in Iowa are cold with lots of snow. The summers are hot.

Corn is one of Iowa's most important crops.

DID YOU KNOW?

The world's steepest and shortest railway is Fenelon Place Elevator in Dubuque, Iowa. It is 296 feet long and climbs 189 feet. It was built in 1882.

In the past

Many people from Europe came and settled in Iowa. Most came from Norway, Germany, the Netherlands, and Denmark. The settlers became farmers. Their traditions are kept alive by people and communities in Iowa today.

Life in Iowa

Nearly all the land in Iowa is still used for farming. Iowa produces about one-tenth of the U.S. food supply. Farmers in Iowa grow corn, soybeans, hay, and oats. They raise many millions of hogs every year. Farmers also raise cattle, sheep, and chickens.

Many of Iowa's factories process foods grown in the state. They make dairy products, popcorn, and oil out of corn.

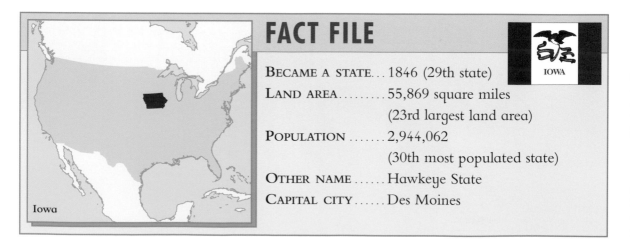

Iowa

FACT FILE

IOWA

BECAME A STATE...	1846 (29th state)
LAND AREA.........	55,869 square miles (23rd largest land area)
POPULATION	2,944,062 (30th most populated state)
OTHER NAME	Hawkeye State
CAPITAL CITY......	Des Moines

Iran

see also: Asia

Iran is a country in southwest Asia. Most of the land is high and flat. There are mountains in the west. Winters in Iran are cold. Summers are much hotter. It rains in the north. The rest of Iran gets very little rain.

Living in Iran

About one-third of the people are farmers. They grow rice and vegetables. Crops have to be watered because there is very little rain.

There are many oilfields in Iran. Most of the oil is sold to other countries. Some people work in factories that make the oil into chemicals.

Some Iranians still live the same way that their ancestors lived hundreds of years ago. They move with herds of sheep and goats to new grazing areas. These people are called nomads.

Most Iranians are followers of Islam. They follow strict laws about how to dress and what to eat and drink.

DID YOU KNOW?

Persia was once the name of Iran. Today the special carpets and rugs made in Iran are still called Persian rugs.

This prayer tower is on a mosque in the city of Isfahan. It is decorated with mosaic tiles. It is from here that people are called to pray five times a day.

Asia

FACT FILE

PEOPLE	Iranians
POPULATION	about 69 million
MAIN LANGUAGE	Farsi (Persian)
CAPITAL CITY	Tehran
MONEY	Rial
HIGHEST MOUNTAIN	Damavand—18,392 feet
LONGEST RIVER	Karun River—450 miles

Iraq

see also: Asia

Iraq is a country in southwest Asia. The Tigris and Euphrates Rivers flow through the middle of Iraq. They flow through flat land. The rivers make marshland as they flow south. There are mountains in the north. Most land in the west is desert. It is wettest in the north.

Living in Iraq

There is good farmland in the Tigris and Euphrates river valleys. About one-third of the people are farmers. They grow vegetables and grain. They raise cattle and goats. There are oilfields in Iraq. Some of the oil is sold to other countries.

In the last 20 years, Iraq has fought wars against neighboring countries Iran and Kuwait. There have also been many problems inside Iraq. In 2003 the United States led an invasion of Iraq. The people of Iraq are now struggling to rebuild their country.

Street vendors sell nuts outside the Golden Mosques in the city of Karbala.

DID YOU KNOW?

A people called Marsh Arabs live in southern Iraq. They live in floating raft houses made of reeds. There are few Marsh Arabs now because the marshes have been drained.

Asia

FACT FILE

PEOPLE	Iraqis
POPULATION	about 25 million
MAIN LANGUAGE	Arabic
CAPITAL CITY	Baghdad
MONEY	New Iraqi dinar
HIGHEST MOUNTAIN	Huji Ibrahim—11,815 feet
LONGEST RIVER	Euphrates River—1,677 miles

Ireland

*see also: Europe,
Northern Ireland*

The Republic of Ireland is a country. It is most of an island in western Europe. The center of Ireland is lowland. There are mountains in the far north and the southwest. The weather is usually mild and wet in winter. It is cool and wet in summer.

Living in Ireland

More than half of the people live in towns and cities. The rest of the people live on farms or in small country towns. More than half of the land is used for grazing cattle. Irish cheese and butter are sold to other countries.

Irish dancing and music are known around the world. Most people in Ireland are Roman Catholic. Two popular sports are Gaelic football and hurling.

Tourists come to Ireland to see the country. Many visit Blarney Castle. They kiss the Blarney stone in the castle wall. A legend says that kissing it will give you the gift of charming people with what you say.

DID YOU KNOW?

St. Patrick's Day is March 17. It is the country's main festival. There is a legend that St. Patrick drove all the snakes out of Ireland about 1,500 years ago.

Europe

FACT FILE

PEOPLE	Irish
POPULATION	almost 4 million
MAIN LANGUAGES	English, Irish Gaelic
CAPITAL CITY	Dublin
MONEY	Euro
HIGHEST MOUNTAIN	Carrantuohill—3,417 feet
LONGEST RIVER	Shannon River—220 miles

Iron Age

see also: Bronze Age, Stone Age

The Iron Age is the time in a country's history when tools and weapons are made from iron. Before this time, tools were made from stone or bronze. People around the world discovered how to make weapons and tools from iron at different times. First, people had to learn how to get iron out of rocks. Then they had to learn how to make things from the iron.

Why was iron important?

Iron is easier to heat than bronze. It does not melt as quickly. It is easier to shape while it is soft. Tools and weapons made from iron are sharper and stronger than those made from bronze.

What came next?

Iron was used for tools and machines until the 1750s. Then people found out that blowing oxygen over very hot iron makes a strong metal. This metal is called steel. People began making things with steel.

KEY DATES

4000 B.C.	People in the Middle East begin to use iron from meteoric rocks.
1500 B.C.	People in the Middle East begin to get iron out of rocks by heating the rocks.
1000 B.C.	People in India and Greece begin to use iron.
800 B.C.	People in Europe begin to use iron.
400 B.C.	People in China begin to use iron.
A.D. 1750s	People begin to use steel.

This Iron Age spearhead was found in France. It fit onto a wooden shaft. It is about 2,500 years old.

Islam

see also: Iran, Saudi Arabia

Islam is a world religion. Its followers are called Muslims. The religion started in Arabia in the Middle East. It was begun by Mohammed in A.D. 622.

Beliefs and teachings

Muslims follow the teachings of their holy book. The holy book is the Koran. They believe the Koran is the word of God. The word of God was given to Mohammed by the archangel Gabriel.

One of the teachings of Islam is that there is only one God and Mohammed is His Prophet. All Muslims must say they believe in God. They must pray and fast, or not eat, at certain times. They must give to the poor. They must go on a journey called a pilgrimage to Mecca. Mecca is the city in Saudi Arabia where Mohammed was born.

Islam today

There are now over one billion Muslims living all over the world. Most Muslims live in the Middle East, Africa, and Asia.

This is a mosque in the Malaysian capital city of Kuala Lumpur. Muslims worship on Fridays at mosques.

Every year more than two million Muslims make the pilgrimage to Mecca to worship and to pray.

DID YOU KNOW?

The Koran is written in the Arabic language. The Arabic word for God is *Allah*. The Islamic name for God is Allah.

Island

see also: Coast, Coral, Ocean

An island is an area of land with water all around it. An island can be in a lake, a sea, or an ocean. It can be very large or very small. Greenland is the largest island in the world.

How islands are made

Some islands are volcanoes that have pushed up from the bottom of the ocean. The Hawaiian Islands in the Pacific Ocean were made this way. Other islands have formed over thousands of years. They formed from living and dead sea animals called coral.

About ten thousand years ago lots of ice melted on Earth. Many areas of land were covered with water. Only the high parts of land were left out of the water. This is another way that many islands were made.

People and islands

Some islands are too small for anyone to live on. There is no drinking water. There is not enough land to grow crops. Islands in hot areas are often popular vacation spots. They have lots of coast. They are good for fishing, watersports, and watching wildlife.

These small islands were once the high parts of a land area. The lighter blue shows where there is land very close to the surface of the water.

This island is off the Alaskan coast. It was formed by a volcano that is still active.

Israel

see also: Asia, Judaism

Israel is a country in the Middle East. It is mostly lowland. There are some mountains to the east and to the north. There is desert to the south. It is hot and dry in the summer. It is cooler and wetter in the winter.

Living in Israel

Most people live in towns and cities. More than half of the land is used for farming and grazing for animals. Farmers use spraying and pipes to get water to their crops.

Israel became a country in 1948. Most of the people living in Israel are Jewish. Israel was formed out of part of the area called Palestine. Not everyone in Palestine wanted the new country. This has caused fighting and wars ever since 1948.

Jerusalem is a very old city. Its history goes back about 5,000 years.

DID YOU KNOW?

Jerusalem is a holy city for Jews, Muslims, and Christians. Many people visit Israel for religious reasons.

Asia

FACT FILE

PEOPLE	Israelis
POPULATION	about 6 million
MAIN LANGUAGES	Hebrew, Arabic
CAPITAL CITY	Jerusalem
MONEY	Shekel
HIGHEST MOUNTAIN	Har Meron—3,965 feet
LONGEST RIVER	Jordan River—200 miles

Italy

see also: Europe; Rome, Ancient

Italy is a country in south Europe. There are mountains in the north and center of Italy. The weather is hot and dry in the summer. It is mild and wet in the winter. There are active volcanoes in the south.

Living in Italy

Italian farmers grow grapes, olives, oranges, wheat, and tomatoes. Italian food is famous all over the world. Spaghetti and pizza are two of its well-known foods. Italy is also famous for its fashion clothing. Big fashion shows are held in cities like Milan.

Vatican City is in the city of Rome. It is the center of the government of the Roman Catholic Church. Many people visit St. Peter's Square in Vatican City.

This is the Leaning Tower of Pisa. Recent work on the foundations has stopped the tower from leaning over any farther.

DID YOU KNOW?

Tourists visit Italy to see the old buildings and works of art. Many tourists visit the Italian city of Venice. Venice is built on islands. It has water canals instead of roads.

Europe

FACT FILE

PEOPLE	Italians
POPULATION	about 58 million
MAIN LANGUAGES	Italian
CAPITAL CITY	Rome
MONEY	Euro
HIGHEST MOUNTAIN	Monte Rosa—15,209 feet
LONGEST RIVER	Po River—404 miles

Jaguar

see also: Cat, Leopard

The jaguar is a mammal. It is a member of the cat family. Jaguars live in Central and South America. Jaguars look a lot like leopards, but jaguars are heavier and stronger. Jaguars also have bigger spots than leopards. The jaguar can climb trees and swim.

JAGUAR FACTS

NUMBER OF KINDS	8
COLOR	yellow with beige and black spots, or totally black
LENGTH	up to 70 inches
HEIGHT	up to 30 inches
WEIGHT	up to 240 lbs.
STATUS	endangered
LIFE SPAN	about 20 years
ENEMIES	snakes, people

Jaguar families

Male and female jaguars live apart. Baby jaguars are called cubs. The female has her cubs in a safe den. She has from one to four cubs at a time. The cubs leave when they are six months old. Then they hunt on their own.

spotted coat to hide in forest shadows

strong teeth to kill and eat food

long tail to balance when climbing

sharp claws for climbing and fighting

soft paws to walk very quietly

a jaguar

MEAT EATER

A jaguar does not need to run far to find food. It hunts by creeping up on animals. It eats big animals such as tapir or deer. It eats small animals such as mice.

This jaguar cub is playing on a fallen tree.

Jamaica

see also: North America

Jamaica is an island country in the Caribbean Sea. Most of Jamaica is covered with mountains and streams. There are lowlands on the south coast. The climate is tropical. It is hot all year. The climate is cooler in the mountains.

Living in Jamaica

About half of all Jamaicans live in rural areas. Many people work with the tourists who vacation in Jamaica.

Sugar cane, bananas, coffee, coconuts, and oranges are grown on farms and plantations. These crops are sold to other countries. Farmers also grow beans, rice, and fruit for local people. Fishermen sell fish to hotels and restaurants.

Music is very popular in Jamaica. Jamaica's reggae music is popular all over the world.

Reggae music began in Jamaica. It developed from a traditional form of Jamaican folk music called mento.

DID YOU KNOW?

The first people who lived on Jamaica were the Arawak Indians. They named the island *Xamayca*. This means "the land of wood and water."

North America

FACT FILE

PEOPLE	Jamaicans
POPULATION	2.7 million
MAIN LANGUAGES	English, Jamaican Creole
CAPITAL CITY	Kingston
MONEY	Jamaican dollar
HIGHEST MOUNTAIN	Blue Mountain Peak—7,404 feet
LONGEST RIVER	Black River—44 miles

Japan

see also: Asia, Earthquake

Japan is a country in southeast Asia. Japan is made up of four large islands and many smaller islands. There are volcanic mountains in the middle of the islands. There are lowlands around the coasts. The north is cold. The south is hot. It rains a lot in Japan.

Living in Japan

Most people in Japan live in the cities. Japan has many factories. Radios, stereos, and televisions are made in Japan. Japan makes more electrical goods than any other country. Japanese-made ships and cars are sold all over the world. Farmers grow rice and fruit. Fishing is also important. Rice and fish are often eaten with soy or spicy sauces.

The Japanese follow many customs from the country's past. There is a special ceremony for serving tea. There are also rules about how people should greet each other.

DID YOU KNOW?

Earthquakes are common in Japan. There was a very big earthquake in the city of Kobe in 1995. More than 5,000 people were killed.

Tokyo is the world's most expensive city in which to live.

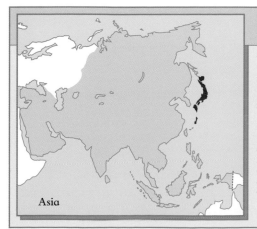

Asia

FACT FILE

PEOPLE . . . . Japanese
POPULATION . . . . about 127 million
MAIN LANGUAGE . . . . . . Japanese
CAPITAL CITY . . . . Tokyo
MONEY . . . . Yen
HIGHEST MOUNTAIN . . Mount Fuji—12,393 feet
LONGEST RIVER . . . . Shinano—228 miles

Jazz

see also: Music, Musical Instrument

Jazz is a form of music. Jazz was started by African Americans about 100 years ago. Jazz is made up of rhythm and improvisation. Improvisation is when jazz musicians make changes in the music while they are playing. Each performance of the same tune can be different.

Traditional and modern jazz

Early jazz is now called traditional jazz. It is usually played by a small group of musicians. They play drums, bass, and piano. Sometimes they also play wind or brass instruments, such as clarinet, trumpet, or trombone. A banjo might be used to play chords. There might be a singer, too.

There are many kinds of modern jazz today. Other places in the world, such as Latin America and Africa, now have their own styles of jazz.

DID YOU KNOW?

The word "cool" is used today to mean something that you like. The word comes from a modern kind of jazz. It is called "cool jazz."

Today's jazz bands might use the same instruments as a pop music band.

LOUIS ARMSTRONG (1900–1971)

Louis Armstrong was born in New Orleans, Louisiana. He played the trumpet, piano, and cornet. He also sang. Armstrong had many exciting ideas about how to change tunes as he played. He also used his voice like an instrument. He would sing sounds instead of words. This is called *scat* singing.

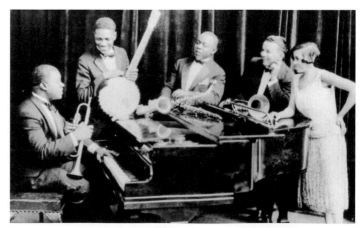

Louis Armstrong is sitting at a piano with one of his early groups, called The Hot Five.

Jefferson, Thomas

see also: Declaration of Independence, Lewis and Clark

Thomas Jefferson was the third president of the United States of America. He helped write the Declaration of Independence.

Young Jefferson

He lived in the colony of Virginia. He inherited a plantation and many slaves. Jefferson became a lawyer. He married Martha Skelton in 1772. They had six children.

Jefferson was a leader in Virginia. When the American Revolution began, the leaders of other colonies asked him to write the Declaration of Independence.

This is a portrait of Thomas Jefferson.

Jefferson becomes president

After the Revolution, Jefferson became vice president in 1797 and then president in 1801. In 1803 he arranged the Louisiana Purchase, which expanded the nation. After he retired, he founded the University of Virginia.

This painting shows the signing of the Declaration of Independence, with Jefferson in the right-hand circle.

DID YOU KNOW?

Thomas Jefferson died on the 50th anniversary of the Declaration of Independence. John Adams, who was president before Jefferson, died the same day.

FACT FILE

DATE OF BIRTH... April 13, 1743

BIRTHPLACE....... Shadwell, Virginia

DATE OF DEATH.. July 4, 1826

PLACE DIED .... Monticello, Virginia

PRESIDENTIAL NUMBER 3

DATES IN OFFICE. 1801–1809

POLITICAL PARTY. Democratic-Republican

VICE PRESIDENTS. Aaron Burr, George Clinton

FIRST LADY .... None

Jellyfish

see also: Invertebrate, Sea Life

A jellyfish is an invertebrate. It is made mostly of soft, jellylike flesh. A jellyfish is shaped like a bell. They are found in all the seas of the world.

Jellyfish families

A jellyfish develops from an egg. It hatches into a polyp. The polyp sticks to the sea bottom. It produces buds. The buds hatch into tiny jellyfish. These tiny jellyfish grow into large, adult jellyfish.

PLANT AND MEAT EATER

Most jellyfish eat plankton. Plankton is made up of tiny plants and animals that float in the sea.

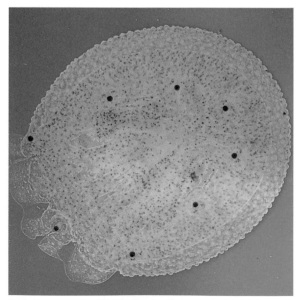

This is a jellyfish polyp. It is in the ocean near the Great Barrier Reef in Australia.

JELLYFISH FACTS

NUMBER OF KINDS	200
COLOR	clear, pink, orange, blue, or other colors
LENGTH	less than an inch to 7 feet
STATUS	common
LIFE SPAN	usually 1 to 3 months
ENEMIES	fish and other sea animals

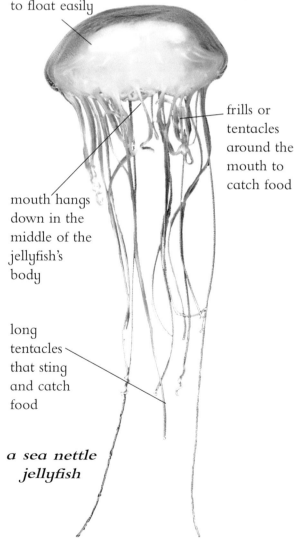

jellylike body to float easily

frills or tentacles around the mouth to catch food

mouth hangs down in the middle of the jellyfish's body

long tentacles that sting and catch food

a sea nettle jellyfish

Jordan

see also: Asia

Jordan is a country in the Middle East. Most of the land is flat desert. There is a river valley in the west. There are mountains in the south. The summer is very hot. The winter is cool with some rain.

Living in Jordan

Most Jordanians live in cities and towns. Only a small amount of the land is good for farming. Some grains, olives, figs, almonds, grapes, apricots, cucumbers, and tomatoes are grown. Some of the fruits and vegetables are sold to other countries.

Tribes called the *Bedouin* live in the deserts. They live in black tents. The Bedouin are nomads. They move from place to place with everything they own.

Jordanians are mostly Arabs. They follow the religion of Islam. Many of their customs and festivals are part of their religion.

These people are wearing traditional clothes. Their headdresses protect them from the sun and blowing sand.

DID YOU KNOW?

The Dead Sea is part of Jordan's border with Israel. The Dead Sea is really a big lake. It is nine times more salty than most oceans. It is easy to float in the Dead Sea.

Asia

FACT FILE

PEOPLE	Jordanians
POPULATION	5.6 million
MAIN LANGUAGE	Arabic
CAPITAL CITY	Amman
MONEY	Jordanian dinar
HIGHEST MOUNTAIN	Jabal Raam—4,923 feet
LONGEST RIVER	Jordan River—200 miles

Judaism

see also: Israel

Judaism is a world religion. Its followers are called Jews. The religion started from the belief in one God. It began in what is now Israel more than 3,000 years ago.

This is the Western Wall in the city of Jerusalem. The wall is all that is left of an old Jewish temple.

Beliefs and teachings

Jews believe that God gave laws called the Ten Commandments to Moses. Moses was a leader of the people of Israel. The Ten Commandments tell people how they should live.

One of the most important Jewish holy books is the Torah. It is written in Hebrew. A Jewish religious leader is called a rabbi.

Judaism today

There are now about 13 million Jews. Most live in the U.S.A., Israel, Britain, and Russia. Six million Jews were killed in Europe during the 1930s and during World War II. The terrible treatment and murder of Jews during this time is called the Holocaust.

A Jewish wedding ceremony is held under a special, decorated canopy.

DID YOU KNOW?

Israel was founded in 1948 as a country for Jews. Most of the holy places named in the Torah are in Israel.

Judicial Branch

see also: Constitution, Executive Branch, Legislative Branch

The judicial branch is one of the three parts of the United States government. The judicial branch is the system of law courts. The job of the law courts is to use the law to solve problems. Some courts decide if a crime has taken place. Other courts settle arguments between two sides.

The Supreme Court is based in this building, in Washington, D.C.

The Supreme Court

The Supreme Court is the most powerful court. If a person doesn't agree with a decision of another court, he or she can appeal to the Supreme Court to hear the case.

DID YOU KNOW?

Before 1954, there was a law in Kansas that stopped a black girl from going to a white school in her neighborhood. The Supreme Court said the law was unconstitutional. It ordered states to get rid of all similar laws. After that decision, African Americans began to gain civil rights in education, jobs, and daily life.

This group photograph of justices of the U.S. Supreme Court was taken in 2003.

The Supreme Court decides whether or not the nation's or states' laws are fair and agree with the Constitution. If the Supreme Court decides a law is unconstitutional, the nation or any state that has that law has to get rid of it. The decision of the Supreme Court is final.

The justices

The Supreme Court has nine judges called justices. One of them is the chief justice. Each justice has one vote in deciding a case. Justices are appointed by the president.

Kangaroo

see also: Australia, Mammal, Marsupial

A kangaroo is a large marsupial mammal. "Marsupial" means that the female has a pouch. This is where she carries her baby. Kangaroos live in Australia. They also live on islands near Australia.

Kangaroo families

A young kangaroo is called a joey. The joey is tiny when it is born. It crawls up the mother's fur. It goes into her pouch. The joey stays in the pouch until it is about eight months old. Female kangaroos and their joeys live in groups. The groups are called herds.

long tail for balancing when jumping, standing, or walking

KANGAROO FACTS

NUMBER OF KINDS	about 50
COLOR	usually brown or gray
LENGTH	2 feet to 10 feet
HEIGHT	up to 7 feet
WEIGHT	up to 155 lbs.
STATUS	common
LIFE SPAN	up to 15 years
ENEMIES	wedgetail eagles, dingoes, people

a female kangaroo and her joey

large ears turn to catch sounds

long back legs to jump as far as 43 feet

female's pouch shelters and protects the joey until the joey is too big to get in and out

This newborn joey is in its mother's pouch. It will drink its mother's milk.

PLANT EATER

A kangaroo eats in the early morning and the early evening during hot weather. It eats grass, leaves, and bark. A kangaroo rests during the day in the shade of a tree.

Kansas

see also: United States of America

Kansas is a state in the central United States of America. Much of Kansas is on the Great Plains. Parts of the state have hills. The summers are warm in Kansas. The winters can be very cold. Sometimes there are tornadoes in spring and dust storms in summer.

In the past

For thousands of years, Native Americans lived in Kansas. Earlier groups, such as the Osage, lived in villages and were farmers. Other Native peoples came later, such as the Comanche. They moved around from place to place.

After 1830, more Native Americans moved to Kansas. They were people from the eastern states who had lost their homelands.

A farmer harvests alfalfa near Dodge City, Kansas.

DID YOU KNOW?

The geographic center of the mainland United States is in northern Kansas. It is about 4 miles west of the town of Lebanon.

Kansas today

Many people in Kansas are farmers. They grow more wheat than any other state in the United States. They also raise cattle. There are many factories in Kansas. Some of them process the food raised in the state. They pack meat and turn wheat into flour. Other factories produce airplanes and railroad cars.

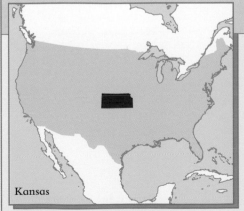

Kansas

FACT FILE

KANSAS

BECAME A STATE...	1861 (34th state)
LAND AREA.........	81,815 square miles (13th largest land area)
POPULATION	2,723,507 (33rd most populated state)
OTHER NAME	Sunflower State
CAPITAL CITY......	Topeka

Kennedy, John F.

see also: Clinton, Bill

John F. Kennedy was the 35th president of the United States of America. He was a young and popular president.

Young Kennedy

He was the second of nine children. He grew up in Massachusetts and New York.

Kennedy graduated from Harvard University in 1940. He joined the U.S. Navy. During World War II, Kennedy saved his crew when their boat was destroyed in the Pacific Ocean. He was elected to the House of Representatives in 1946. He became a senator in 1953.

Kennedy inspired Americans with new hope.

Kennedy becomes president

Kennedy was elected president in 1960. As president, Kennedy encouraged space exploration. He supported civil rights for African Americans. Kennedy was shot and killed while on a trip to Dallas, Texas.

Kennedy talks to the leader of the U.S.S.R., Nikita Khrushchev.

DID YOU KNOW?

John F. Kennedy started the Peace Corps in 1961. The group sends Americans to help people in poor countries.

FACT FILE

DATE OF BIRTH... May 29, 1917
BIRTHPLACE....... Brookline, Massachusetts
DATE OF DEATH.. November 22, 1963
PLACE DIED .... Dallas, Texas
PRESIDENTIAL
NUMBER 35
DATES IN OFFICE. 1961–1963
POLITICAL PARTY. Democratic
VICE PRESIDENT .. Lyndon B. Johnson
FIRST LADY .... Jacqueline Kennedy

Kentucky

see also: United States of America

Kentucky is a state in the eastern United States of America. There are mountains in the east of the state. In the north-central Bluegrass region are grassy hills. There are swamps in the southwest of the state. Kentucky has many miles of running water and lakes.

Kentucky is known for breeding horses on farms like this one.

Life in Kentucky

Kentucky has many riches underground. Its natural resources include coal, oil, and gas. Mammoth Cave in Kentucky is the world's longest cave system. It has more than 350 miles (560 kilometers) of underground passages. The world's biggest store of gold is also underground in Kentucky. It is held in the gold vault at Fort Knox military base.

DID YOU KNOW?

Many people in the Bluegrass region of Kentucky breed horses. The Kentucky Derby is a famous horse race. It takes place every year in Louisville.

Most people in Kentucky live in cities. The two largest cities are Lexington and Louisville. People in Kentucky work in offices, stores, and factories. They also work in coal mines and at gas and oil fields. Farmers in the state raise tobacco, corn, and soybeans.

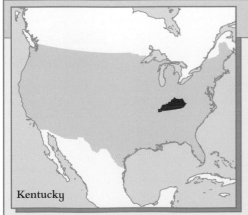

Kentucky

FACT FILE

BECAME A STATE	1792 (15th state)
LAND AREA	39,728 square miles (36th largest land area)
POPULATION	4,117,827 (26th most populated state)
OTHER NAME	Bluegrass State
CAPITAL CITY	Frankfort

Kenya

see also: Africa

Kenya is a country in East Africa. There are hot lowlands and coastal areas in the east. There is higher land with mountains in the west. The Rift Valley runs through Kenya from north to south. The north is hot desert. The rainy season is in April and May.

Living in Kenya

Most Kenyans live in the rural areas. They work on farms. They raise animals. They grow food to eat. Coffee and tea are grown on big farms. These two crops are sold to other countries.

The people come from 40 African tribes. The national motto is *Harambee*. This means "Let's all pull together."

These men of the Samburu tribe are performing a traditional war dance.

DID YOU KNOW?

Many wild animals roam in Kenya's national parks. Tourists go on "camera safaris." The tourists travel through the parks and take photographs of the animals.

Africa

FACT FILE

PEOPLE	Kenyans
POPULATION	about 32 million
MAIN LANGUAGES	Swahili, English
CAPITAL CITY	Nairobi
MONEY	Kenyan shilling
HIGHEST MOUNTAIN	Mount Kenya—17,063 feet
LONGEST RIVER	Tana River—453 miles

King, Martin Luther, Jr.

see also: Holiday

Dr. Martin Luther King Jr. was a civil rights leader. He helped African Americans to have the same rights as white people.

Peaceful protests

King was born on January 15, 1929, in Atlanta, Georgia. When he was a child, African Americans were treated differently from white people.

King became a minister in Montgomery, Alabama. In 1955, the city's African Americans began a protest against the bus system. King led the protest. The bus company had to get rid of "whites only" sections on buses.

King led many peaceful protests and marches. In 1963, he led the March on Washington for Jobs and Freedom. Over 200,000 people took part.

Dr. King waves to the crowd during the March on Washington.

Death in Memphis

King helped African Americans gain civil rights. In 1968, he went to Memphis, Tennessee, to support black workers there. On April 4, King was shot and killed outside his motel room.

Dr. King worked to change unfair laws without using violence.

KEY DATES

1929 .. Martin Luther King Jr. is born.
1955 .. Montgomery bus boycott begins.
1963 .. March on Washington.
1964 .. King wins the Nobel Peace Prize.
1968 .. King dies.

Kiwi

see also: Bird, New Zealand

A kiwi is a bird that cannot fly. It lives only in New Zealand. A kiwi can run fast. It has feathers that look like hairs.

Kiwi families

The female kiwi lays two eggs. She lays them in a nest hole or in a hollow log. The male sits on the eggs for eleven weeks. This is longer than any other bird sits on eggs. The young kiwi are called chicks. The chicks have all their feathers when they hatch. They can see, too. The chicks leave the nest after one week. They go off on their own.

long beak for reaching worms

sensitive nostrils for smelling food

strong legs for running and kicking in fights

KIWI FACTS

NUMBER OF KINDS	3
COLOR	brownish-gray
HEIGHT	14 inches
LENGTH	20 inches
WEIGHT	up to 5 lbs.
STATUS	common
LIFE SPAN	not known
ENEMIES	rats, stoats, ferrets

a common kiwi

PLANT, INSECT, AND MEAT EATER

A kiwi sleeps in the daytime. It walks around at night looking for insects, worms, berries, fruit, and lizards to eat.

This female brown kiwi has just laid this egg. The egg is very large compared to her size.

Knight

see also: Middle Ages

A knight was a fighting man. He fought while riding a horse. This was in Europe in the Middle Ages. Knights fought for a king or queen. They also fought for the most important person where they lived.

What did a knight wear?

Knights wore armor to fight. Armor was made from pieces of metal. The metal was shaped to fit different parts of the body. It was difficult to hurt a knight when he was covered from head to foot in metal. Armor was very heavy. Knights could not move fast. Their horses had to be very strong.

A knight fought with a lance. A lance is a long pole with sharp metal on the end. Knights also had swords and daggers.

Who could be a knight?

Knights were men from important families. Boys lived in a knight's home. The boys worked as pages. The pages fetched and carried things for the knight. They served his food. A page became a squire when he was older. Squires trained to be knights. Then they became knights in a special ceremony.

Knights were not needed for fighting any more after about A.D. 1600.

Armor had many parts. These pictures show the layers of clothes a knight needed to put on.

Koala

see also: Australia, Mammal, Marsupial

A koala is a marsupial mammal. Marsupial means that the female has a pouch for her young. Koalas look like small bears. They live only in Australia. A koala lives most of its life in the trees. It can walk or swing from tree to tree. A koala never drinks. It gets all the water it needs when it eats eucalyptus leaves.

Koala families

A newborn koala is less than one inch long. It is blind and hairless. It climbs through its mother's fur to her pouch. It drinks her milk while it is in the pouch. The baby is six months old when it leaves the pouch. Then it moves onto its mother's back.

KOALA FACTS

NUMBER OF KINDS...	1
COLOR	gray and white
LENGTH	up to 30 inches
WEIGHT	up to 26 lbs.
STATUS	common
LIFE SPAN	about 15 to 20 years
ENEMIES	people who destroy eucalyptus forests

long fingers and strong claws for climbing trees

thick fur for keeping warm at night

a koala

A female koala carries her baby on her back until it is fully grown.

PLANT EATER

A koala is a very fussy eater. The only food it eats is the leaves from twelve kinds of eucalyptus tree. A koala feeds at night. It moves from one tree to another to find enough leaves to eat.

Kuwait

see also: Asia, Desert

Kuwait is a country in the Middle East. It is all flat lowland. Kuwait has a coast in the east. It is mostly very hot desert. It is a bit cooler from October to March. There is very little rain.

Living in Kuwait

Nearly everybody in Kuwait lives in cities or towns. Kuwait City is very modern. It has lots of tall buildings. The only big industry is the production of oil and natural gas. There are thousands of oil wells.

No food can be grown in Kuwait. Shrimp and fish are caught in the sea. All other food is bought from other countries. Drinking water is made by taking the salt out of the sea water. This is called desalination. It is done in special factories.

These men are building a dhow. A dhow is a traditional Arab sailboat.

DID YOU KNOW?

Kuwait is one of the Gulf States. This is the name given to all the countries that are around the Persian Gulf.

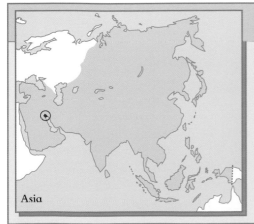

Asia

FACT FILE

PEOPLE	Kuwaitis
POPULATION	over 2 million
MAIN LANGUAGES	Arabic
CAPITAL CITY	Kuwait
MONEY	Kuwaiti dinar
HIGHEST MOUNTAIN	no land above 650 feet
LONGEST RIVER	no rivers

Ladybug

see also: Beetle, Insect

A ladybug is a brightly-colored, spotted beetle. They are found in most parts of the world, but not in very cold places. Ladybugs are also called ladybirds.

Ladybug families

A ladybug egg hatches into a larva. The larva is a gray grub. It has black, red, blue, or green spots. A fully grown larva spins a special covering. It forms a pupa. Inside the pupa, it changes into an adult ladybug.

LADYBUG FACTS	
NUMBER OF KINDS	5,000
COLOR	brightly colored with black, yellow, or red spots
LENGTH	less than one inch
STATUS	common
LIFE SPAN	less than a year
ENEMIES	birds, chemical pesticides

different kinds of ladybugs have different numbers and colors of spots

a ladybug

hard covers to protect the wings underneath

INSECT EATER

A ladybug is a friend to gardeners and farmers. It eats greenflies and other insects that damage plants.

These young ladybugs are gathering together in a swarm.

Lake

see also: River, Valley

A lake is an area of water. It has land all around it. Some lakes are so big that they are called seas. A very small lake is called a pond.

How lakes are made

There are two ways many lakes have formed. One way is from the ice that covered the earth a long, long time ago. Sheets of ice dug deep holes in the ground. Lakes formed in these holes. Another way lakes have formed is from cracks in the earth's surface. These cracks are called fault lines. The cracks can fill up with water to make a lake.

There is fresh water in most lakes. Fresh water rivers sometimes flow into lakes. Then the rivers flow out again. Some lakes are very salty. This is because rivers that flow into the lake are carrying salt from rocks.

People and lakes

Large boats on lakes carry goods. People also make special lakes to store water. These lakes are called reservoirs. People use lakes for fishing, boating, and watersports. Lakes are also important homes for wildlife.

The Great Salt Lake in Utah is very salty. Salty rivers flow into it.

DID YOU KNOW?

The deepest lakes in Africa are along a huge fault line called the Great Rift Valley. Water filled the hollows along the crack where the land sunk. This made the lakes.

Loch Ness in Scotland is a lake formed along a fault line. It is famous for the Loch Ness monster that some people believe lives there.

Language

see also: Alphabet, Communication

Language is how people communicate with each other. People use language to tell others what they want, think, or feel. Language is both spoken words and written words. Today, there are about 6,000 languages in the world.

Language around the world

More people speak Chinese than any other language. Many people speak English, Hindi, Spanish, French, Russian, and Arabic. There are about 1,300 languages in Africa. All of them probably started from just four languages. Languages change over time.

English

The English language began to spread around the world about 400 years ago. People traveled to new places. They spread their language as they traveled. Now more than 320 million people speak English. Many people also learn English as their second language.

Chinese }	魚
Japanese }	
Dutch	VIS
Spanish	PEZ
Greek	ΨΑΡΙ
Russian	РЫБА
Finnish	KALA
Swedish	FISK
English	FISH
German	FISCH
Italian	PESCE
French	POISSON
Turkish	BALIK

Here is the word fish in thirteen languages. This word is nearly the same in some languages. In other languages, the word looks very different.

This teacher uses sign language to read a story to children who are deaf.

DID YOU KNOW?

Sign language is a special way to communicate. People use their hands to make symbols or spell out words in this language. Sign language was invented for people who cannot hear or speak.

Laser

see also: Bar Code, Computer, Light

A laser is a machine. It makes a ray of light. Lasers have many uses. Tiny lasers are used in CD players and cable TV. Powerful lasers are used in medical operations.

How do lasers work?

All beams of light carry energy. All of the energy in a laser light is in a very narrow beam. The beam makes a tiny spot. This tiny spot is very hot in a powerful laser.

How is a laser used?

Some laser beams carry TV and radio signals. Others carry telephone messages. Many signals can be sent a long way through cables.

CD players use laser beams. The beam shines on the CD and bounces off it. This light is the code for the music. Nothing touches the disc. The disc does not wear out. Doctors use lasers like knives to cut during operations. Laser beams can also burn away tumors.

The red lines are laser beams. Laser beams stay narrow. Regular light spreads out.

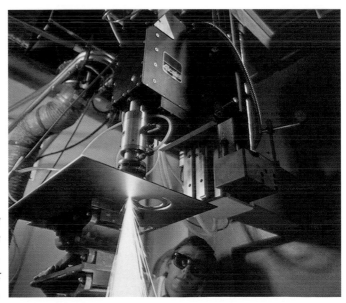

This laser machine is held by a robot arm. The arm moves and shoots out laser beams. The beams make a clean cut through metal.

Leaf

see also: Photosynthesis, Plant

A leaf is part of a plant. It makes the plant's food. Green plants grow almost everywhere except where it is very cold or very dry. Different plants have different shaped leaves.

Life of a leaf

A bud forms on the stem of a plant. The bud opens. A new leaf and stem begin to grow. The leaves of some plants live for years. The leaves of many other plants die after several months.

People and animals could not live without leaves. Many animals eat leaves, grass, and plants. Meat eaters eat the plant-eating animals. People eat the leaves of some plants. Some leaves are used as medicines. Tea is made from the leaves of tea plants.

narrow tube-like veins carry water to the leaf and take food away from the leaf

chlorophyll gives the leaf its green color and turns light into food

stem joins the leaf to the rest of the plant

The African raffia palm has the largest leaves of any tree. The leaves grow up to 65 feet long.

DID YOU KNOW?

Some leaves change color in the autumn. Then they fall off the trees and plants. This is because the water supply to the leaves has stopped. Then the green chlorophyll stops forming and other colors appear.

Lebanon

see also: Asia

Lebanon is a country in the Middle East. It has two mountain ranges. There is good farm land between the mountain ranges. There is a narrow coast in the west. Summers are hot. Winters are cool. Lebanon gets some rain.

Living in Lebanon

Most Lebanese live in the cities and towns. There is some industry. Things are made from chemicals, gold, and silver. Farmers grow fruits, olives, grapes, and tobacco. Olives are a favorite snack in Lebanon.

People have lived in Lebanon for thousands of years. In recent times, Lebanon has had about 50 years of war. There has been fighting between Arabs, Palestinians, and Israelis.

Beirut has a natural harbor. It has been used by ships for thousands of years.

DID YOU KNOW?

The tree called the Cedar of Lebanon has been a symbol of Lebanon for about 2,000 years. The tree symbol is on Lebanon's flag. Some Cedars of Lebanon are more than 3,000 years old.

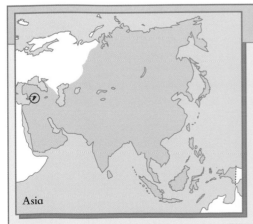

Asia

FACT FILE

PEOPLE	Lebanese
POPULATION	3.7 million
MAIN LANGUAGES	Arabic, French
CAPITAL CITY	Beirut
MONEY	Lebanese pound
HIGHEST MOUNTAIN	Qurnat as Sawdā'–10,135 feet
LONGEST RIVER	Litani River–90 miles

Legend

see also: Literature, Myth, Story

A legend is a story that has been handed down through the years. The story is often about heroes or exciting events. Legends can have magic or supernatural things in them, but the stories are always about human beings. This makes legends different from myths. Myths are about gods or supernatural beings. Every country in the world has its own legends.

Real and pretend

Many legends are based on real people. The English legends of King Arthur may be about a real person. The legends say that King Arthur had a magic sword. They say he had a magician called Merlin. The legends also say that King Arthur and his knights sat around a round table. Some of these things may be true. Some of these things may be pretend. Pieces are added to legends as the stories are told again and again.

Johnny Appleseed is a hero in American legends.

JOHNNY APPLESEED

Johnny Appleseed was the nickname of a real person. His name was John Chapman. He was an early American settler in the 1800s. He planted apple trees, so people called him Appleseed. Many of the stories about him and his family are pretend.

This picture is 600 years old. It shows King Arthur and his knights.

Legislative Branch

see also: Constitution, Executive Branch, Judicial Branch

The legislative branch is one of the three parts of the United States government. The job of the legislative branch is to make laws.

Congress

Congress is the main part of the legislative branch. The legislative branch also has parts that help Congress, such as the Library of Congress and the printing office.

The word "congress" means meeting. Congress meets throughout the year. Congress decides and passes laws for the nation. It also decides how to spend the nation's money. Congress has two parts, or houses. They are the Senate and the House of Representatives.

This photograph shows a joint session of Congress in September 2004. "Joint session" means that both the members of the House of Representatives and the members of the Senate are there.

Both houses have to approve a new law before it passes. All members of Congress are elected by the people.

The Houses

The Senate has 100 members, two from each state. It approves the president's decisions about foreign treaties and who he or she puts in important jobs. The House of Representatives has 435 members. Every state has at least one representative. States with the biggest population have the most representatives.

The U.S. Capitol building in Washington, D.C. is where Congress meets.

Leopard

see also: Cat, Jaguar, Mammal

The leopard is a mammal. It is a member of the cat family. Leopards live in Africa and southern Asia. Most leopards live on grassy plains. Leopards also live in very hot areas and in high mountains.

LEOPARD FACTS

NUMBER OF KINDS....	7
COLOR......	yellow with black and brown spots, or totally black
LENGTH.....	up to 6 feet
HEIGHT.....	up to 28 inches
WEIGHT.....	up to 200 lbs.
STATUS......	endangered
LIFE SPAN...	about 12 years
ENEMIES.....	people

long tail for balance

spotted coat for hiding

the leopard

strong teeth for killing and eating food

soft paws for walking very quietly

sharp claws for climbing and fighting

Leopard families

Adult leopards live by themselves. The female makes a home called a lair. This is where she has her babies. The babies are called cubs. The mother moves her lair every few days to keep her young cubs safe. The cubs stay with their mother for about two years.

MEAT EATER

A leopard catches antelope, baboons, and warthogs. It will also eat smaller animals and birds. The leopard carries its food up into trees. This keeps its food out of the reach of lions and vultures.

A female leopard cares for her cub.

Lewis and Clark

see also: Jefferson, Thomas; Sacagawea

Meriwether Lewis and William Clark were explorers. They explored the western part of the United States.

The expedition

In 1802, President Thomas Jefferson and Lewis planned an expedition. At that time, the United States was only in the eastern part of North America. Then in 1803 the United States bought the Louisiana Territory from France. The expedition would explore that land and find a route to the Pacific Ocean.

Lewis asked William Clark to help him lead the expedition. Lewis and Clark assembled boats, equipment, and men. They named their expedition "The Corps of Discovery."

Lewis and Clark are shown meeting Native Americans on their journey.

The Corps started in May 1804 along the Missouri River. In October, the men built a fort among the Hidatsa and Mandan people of North Dakota. They spent the winter there. In spring, Lewis and Clark set off again. They met many more Native American peoples. They saw new animals and plants. They were helped by a Native American woman called Sacagawea.

Reaching the ocean

The journey was dangerous and difficult. In November 1805, the Corps finally reached the Pacific Ocean. They built a winter fort among the Clatsop people. In the spring of 1806, Lewis and Clark led their men home. The expedition arrived back in St. Louis on September 23, 1806.

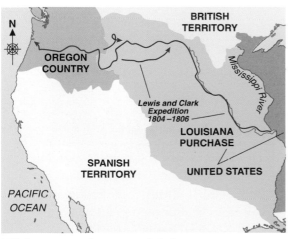

This map shows which way Lewis and Clark went.

DID YOU KNOW?

Lewis and Clark's expedition took more than two years. In that time, they traveled 4,350 miles, there and back.

Liberty Bell

see also: Declaration of Independence

The Liberty Bell is a large, old bell. Liberty is another word for freedom. The Liberty Bell is a symbol of freedom for the United States of America.

About the Bell

The Liberty Bell came from England. It is made mostly of copper. It weighs about 2,000 pounds (900 kilograms). The bell was made for the colony of Pennsylvania. The Pennsylvania government ordered it in 1751 to celebrate 50 years of religious freedom in the colony. On its side are these words from the Bible: "Proclaim liberty throughout all the land unto all the inhabitants thereof." The bell was hung in the bell tower of the Pennsylvania State House in Philadelphia, now called Independence Hall.

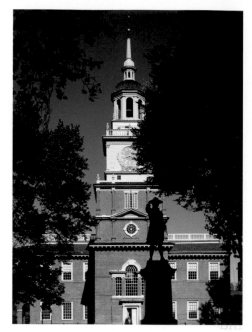

Independence Hall, Philadelphia, is where you can visit the Liberty Bell.

A new kind of liberty

The colony of Pennsylvania was not really free. It was under British rule. In 1776, British colonists declared independence. They founded the United States of America. The Declaration of Independence was agreed in Independence Hall. The Liberty Bell rang out after the Declaration was made.

Today, the Liberty Bell represents liberty for the whole nation. Millions of people come to see it every year.

Liberty Bell

DID YOU KNOW?

The Liberty Bell made in England cracked soon after it arrived. Two Philadelphia craftspeople made a new bell from the same metal. They had to do it twice to get it right. The new bell cracked too. The crack is still there today.

Libya

see also: Africa, Desert

Libya is a country in northern Africa. Libya is almost all desert. The land is mostly flat. It has a few low mountains. The coast is cooler and sometimes has rain.

Living in Libya

Most Libyans live in cities on the coast. Oil and natural gas were discovered in Libya in 1959. This made Libya a rich country.

Farmers in the north grow dates, olives, citrus fruits, grapes, and wheat. Sheep, goats, cattle, and camels graze where there is enough grass for them to eat.

There are no rivers that flow all year round. The people need more water for farming, drinking, and washing. Libya is working to bring water from one end of the country to the other.

These Tuareg men in southern Libya are performing a traditional dance.

DID YOU KNOW?

The highest temperature ever recorded was in Libya in 1922. It was 136°F.

Africa

FACT FILE

PEOPLE	Libyans
POPULATION	5.6 million
MAIN LANGUAGES	Arabic, Berber, Italian, English
CAPITAL CITY	Tripoli
MONEY	Libyan dinar
HIGHEST MOUNTAIN	Bette Peak–7,503 feet
LONGEST RIVER	Rivers flow only when it rains.

Lice

see also: Insect

Lice are small insects. They have no wings. They have very fat bodies. Lice live in the clothes, hair, feathers, and fur of people and animals.

Lice families

An adult female louse lays tiny eggs. The eggs are called nits. The nits take a week or two to hatch. Lice move from person to person. Head lice spread quickly wherever there are lots of people. Lice spread quickly in camps and schools. They can make the skin and head itch.

LICE FACTS

NUMBER OF KINDS	3,300
COLOR	brown or yellow-brown
SIZE	much less than one inch
STATUS	common
LIFE SPAN	one month
ENEMIES	special chemicals called insecticides

tube for sucking up blood

body swells up with blood

a human head louse

claws for gripping hair and fur

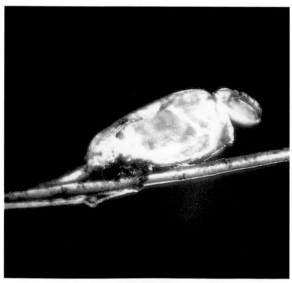

A head louse egg sticks to hair.

MEAT EATER

Lice poke a hole in the skin of their victims. Then they suck up blood. There are different types of lice. Some types of lice live on humans. Some lice live on other mammals. Some lice live on birds.